Hartmut Wilke

Turtles
Everything about Purchase, Care, Nutrition, and Behavior

Filled with Full-color Photographs

Illustrations by Robert Fischer

2 CONTENTS

WHAT
TURTLES ARE LIKE

- Solitary by nature.
- Hard–shelled but very sensitive to touch.
- Have good vision and a keen sense of smell.
- Love to bask in the sun.
- Many species hibernate.
- Have a "beak" instead of teeth.
- Learn quickly.
- In the wild, may live as long as 120 years.

Turtles have lived on the earth since the time of the dinosaurs, and turtles continue to fascinate humans. Like the crocodiles, they are one of the oldest families of the animal kingdom, surviving as messengers from the past. In ancient times, the earth's climate was much warmer than it is now, and the turtles of today are still more or less adapted to those conditions. Their natural habitat lies primarily in the world's tropical and subtropical regions. However, some species have been able to adapt to the changing seasons of North America, Europe, and Australia by hibernating during the cold of winter; examples are the wood turtle (*Clemmys insculpta*) and the painted turtle (*Chrysemys picta*). If you choose to keep a turtle, you should definitely know all about its basic needs and see that they are met. A healthy, lively turtle can give you pleasure for many years.

6 FACTORS IN YOUR DECISION

1 Are you allergic to animal hair? No problem; research has shown that turtles do not trigger allergies in humans.

2 Do you have a yard or garden? Many turtles enjoy fresh outdoor air in the summertime. A patio or balcony with a southern or southwest exposure will also serve this purpose.

3 Turtles of many tropical species are highly sensitive to cold and should be kept indoors except in very warm and sunny weather (see profiles, pages 10–17).

4 Keep in mind that a large aquarium for an aquatic turtle is quite heavy. A medium-sized tank with 52 gallons (200 liters) of water, together with its stand and accessories, weighs about 550 pounds (250 kg).

5 Providing the right environment for a semiaquatic or aquatic turtle requires specific equipment that can be expensive but essential if your pet turtle is to thrive. Tropical species often spend their entire lives in the aquarium or terrarium.

6 Do you have a suitable site for an indoor aquarium? Drafts and constant vibrations (from stereo systems, for example) are harmful to turtles.

7 Do you have access to a cold cellar or unheated basement for overwintering your turtle? Depending on your location, garden ponds, attics, tool sheds, greenhouses, and balconies may not be suitable places for turtles to hibernate.

8 Sick turtles must be cared for by a veterinarian who is familiar with their special treatment needs. You should locate such a specialist ahead of time, so that your turtle can get help in an emergency.

9 Are there other pets in the household? Before you buy a turtle, consider whether the animals will get along.

10 Plan ahead to find someone who can care for your turtle in case you are sick or away from home for an extended time.

One or Two?

Although water turtles may be considered solitary creatures, they do bask together in large aggregations. In the wild, they pair up during the mating season, but these are opportunistic pairings that do not last for long.

One requirement for keeping a breeding pair is to be sure of the sex of your two turtles. You also need an aquaterrarium of appropriate size, facilities to keep the two turtles separated if they do not get along, an egg deposition site, a way to incubate the eggs, and a separate aquarium for raising the young (see HOW-TO, page 46). It can be a matter of luck to choose a breeding pair from young turtles, because at this age males and females are hard to distinguish. If two young males grow up together, unfortunately one may start to bully the other as they reach maturity.

Males and females of different species may tolerate each other, but their mating rarely produces offspring. Furthermore, for the sake of species protection, it's preferable to avoid crosses between different species.

Male or Female?

If you keep only one turtle, it really doesn't matter whether it's male or female; their day-to-day behavior is almost the same. If you definitely want one of each, or a suitable mate for your turtle, it's best to choose from nearly full-grown or adult turtles. The younger the turtle, the more difficult it is for someone who is not an expert to distinguish between males and females. In many species of turtles, the male's plastron is more concave than the female's. Male turtles also usually have a somewhat longer tail, broader at the base, with the vent closer to the end of the tail. In many fresh water species, even half-grown males can be identified quite clearly by their front claws, which are obviously longer than those of females. Males of some species are also significantly smaller than the females.

ACQUIRING A TURTLE AND GETTING IT SETTLED

The key to successful turtle care is a thorough knowledge of the habits and needs of these primeval reptiles. Before you bring your new pet home, you should be familiar with its specific requirements so that you'll be ready to provide the proper care right from the start.

The Natural History of Semiaquatic and Aquatic Turtles

Water-dwelling turtles come in all sizes, from the immense to the relatively tiny. The largest and heaviest sea turtle is the leatherback turtle. It is more than 5 feet (1.5 m) long and weighs as much as 1,800 pounds (800 kg). Lazing in the sunshine at the surface of tropical ocean waters, this massive creature is an impressive sight. Sea turtles have a flat shell and legs that have evolved into paddles, enabling them to swim and dive extremely well in the ocean. By contrast, the smallest aquatic turtles, such as the spotted turtles, are only 4–5 inches (10–12 cm) long and weigh only about 4 ounces (120 g). Fossils from the Mesozoic era show that turtles lived on the earth as long as 180 million years ago, in the time of the dinosaurs. Some such fossils have been found in Germany, at the edge of the Harz mountain range. These turtles were more than 20 inches (0.5 m) long. The mouth of the fossilized turtles was found to contain small knobby teeth, overgrown by the gums. Vestiges of teeth could also still be clearly identified on the jaws. The shell was flat and resembled the shells of today.

In some ways, however, time has brought evolutionary changes. Today's turtles no longer have teeth, but horny jaws with jagged edges that they use to tear their food. The turtle's shell has also undergone a wide variety of adaptations. The soft-shelled turtle, for example, no longer has a shell in the conventional sense; its body is protected only by a tough, elastic skin. Only a small patch of bony shell remains on the turtle's underside (see page 14). Other species of turtles, such as the big-headed turtle, have a hard skull roof; as a result, it is no longer necessary or possible for them to retract the head into the shell for protection. Still other turtles have joints and hinges in their shell. After pulling in their head and limbs, these turtles can close their houses up tight (see sliders, page 11).

A lively swimmer, the Australian snake-necked turtle comes up for a breath of air.

PROFILES:

Wood turtle.

Common Musk Turtle (Stinkpot).

Wood Turtle

Clemmys insculpta
Size: Female 5 inches (13 cm), male up to 9
inches (23 cm). Distribution: United States and
Canada. Protected in all states. Habitat: Bogs,
woodlands, and pasture edges. Behavior: Active
by day. Can climb over wire-netting fence 6 ft
(2 m) high. Intelligent. Care: Terrarium or
outdoor enclosure with hide box; air temperature
should be 65–80°F. Good candidate for outdoor
enclosure if temperatures permit. Diet: Beetles,
snails, worms, berries, and fruit. Hibernation:
Yes, breeding is planned beginning in first
winter. Hibernates under water or rarely
burrows under the soil on land.

Common Musk Turtle (Stinkpot)

Sternotherus odoratus
Size: Up to 6 inches (15 cm). Distribution:
United States (Florida) to southern Canada.
Habitat: Still waters, abundant vegetation, and
gently sloping shores. Behavior: Active day and
night; hearty eater. Care: Semiaquatic terrarium
and garden pond; provide water temperature of
68–77°F (20–25°C) for specimens from the
northern U.S., 73–82°F (23–28°C) for those
from the southern U.S. Air temperature 75–82°F
(24–28°C). May be kept in a garden pond spring
and summer when temperatures permit. Diet:
Carnivorous. Hibernation: Depends on place of
origin. Winter cooling generally sufficient.
Special notes: Poor swimmer. Place roots or
stones under water to help the turtle propel
itself along. Even sisal rope ends will do, but
they must be thick, about 2.5 inches (6 cm) in
diameter; the turtle might become tangled in
thinner lengths and drown. In garden pond, be
sure the shore is gently sloping for easy exit
from the water. These turtles secrete a foul-
smelling *musk* when disturbed.

The Mississippi map turtle is a riverine species.

Red-eared slider.

Mississippi Map Turtle.

Red-eared Slider

Trachemys scripta elegans
Size: Up to 10 inches (25 cm). Distribution: Southern United States, east and west of the Mississippi. [*1998 Wilke Turtles and Tortoises, Americanized;* introduced worldwide] Habitat: Quiet waters having abundant vegetation and warming quickly in the sun's heat. Behavior: Active by day; enjoys basking; lively swimmer. Care: Aquarium and garden pond; in aquarium, water temperature 79–82°F (26–28°C), air temperature 79–90°F (26–32°C). May be kept in a garden pond from June to August. Diet: Juveniles carnivorous (trout chow, minnows, earthworms, dry cat kibble). Adults largely herbivorous. Hibernation: Not necessary, even to breed. Caution: Can be kept year-round in the garden pond only if temperatures are above 70°F. Special note: The red-eared slider does best alone, except when breeding is the goal. Even breeding pairs will not get along if their quarters are cramped. Species requiring similar conditions: Cumberland slider, *Trachemys scripta troosti*, to 10 inches (25 cm) long; hieroglyphic river cooter, *Pseudemys concinna hieroglyphica,* to 16 inches (40 cm) long.

Mississippi Map Turtle

Graptemys pseudogeographica kohnii
Size: Up to 10 inches (25 cm); males, only up to 5 inches (13 cm). Distribution: Southern United States. Habitat: A riverine species; may be found in oxbow ponds with abundant vegetation and plentiful insects and fish. Behavior: Active by day. Care: Aquarium with an island for sunning (see page 25); water temperature 72–82°F (22–28°C), air temperature 72–82°F (22–28°C). Place in garden pond when temperatures permit. Diet: Chiefly insectivorous/carnivorous; may eat a little vegetation. Likes snails, mollusks, worms, crustaceans, and insects. Hibernation: Not needed. Species requiring similar conditions: The rarely available caspians: the black Caspian turtle, *Mauremys caspica leprosa*. Size, up to 10 inches (25 cm). Spain, Portugal, and Algeria. Caspian turtle, *Mauremys caspica caspica*. Size, up to 10 inches (25 cm). False map turtle, *Graptemys pseudogeographica*. Size, up to 10 inches (25 cm). Four subspecies; inhabits southern U.S. Found south of the Caspian Sea; three subspecies.

PROFILES:

Spotted turtle.

Reeves' turtle.

Spotted Turtle

Clemmys guttata

Size: Up to 5 inches (12 cm). Distribution:
Eastern and northeastern United States.
Habitat: Small, marshy meadow and woodland
ponds. Behavior: Active by day, when the water
is warm enough. Needs shallow water; likes to
bask in the sun when the water is cold. Care:
Semiaquatic terrarium and outdoor enclosure;
water temperature 72–81°F (22–27°C), air
temperature 72–82°F (22–28°C). May enjoy a
garden pond when temperatures permit. Diet:
Carnivorous. Hibernation: Yes, from the first
winter. Provide winter cooling the second year
to breed this species. Special notes: Males have
brown eyes, females yellow. Length of
hibernation varies, depending on place of
origin (broad distribution north to south).
Watch its behavior closely during hibernation
(see page 34).

Reeves' Turtle

Chinemys reevesii

Size: Up to 7 inches (17 cm). Distribution:
Indonesia, Japan, southeastern China. Habitat:
Calm fresh and brackish bodies of water.
Behavior: Active by day. Care: Shallow aquarium and garden pond; both should provide a
way to climb out of the water because this
turtle is a poor swimmer. Garden pond from
June to August, but only on hot days when the
water temperature reaches 80°F (27°C),
because the species sold in pet shops generally
come from the more southern regions. Air
temperature 75–82°F (24–28°C). Diet:
Carnivorous. Hibernation: No. Species requiring
similar conditions: Red-bellied short-necked
turtle, *Emydura albertisii,* from New Guinea
and Australia (see photograph, page 18); mixed
diet. This colorful semiaquatic turtle reproduces
readily in captivity and has become a popular
choice among turtle lovers recently.

A young snake-necked turtle.

Malayan box turtle.

Common Snake-necked Turtle

Chelodina longicollis
<u>Size:</u> Up to 12 inches (30 cm). <u>Distribution:</u>
Eastern Australia. <u>Habitat:</u> Still and slowly
flowing water, shallow shore. In rainy season,
also temporarily on land. <u>Behavior:</u> Active by
day; lively swimmer; very likely to bite during
mating period. <u>Care:</u> Especially spacious
aquarium; water temperature 73–82°F
(23–28°C), air temperature 75–82°F (24–28°C).
<u>Diet:</u> Carnivorous. <u>Hibernation:</u> No. <u>Special
notes:</u> This turtle, a member of the side-neck
family, turns its head and its relatively long
neck and tucks it under its carapace for
protection.

Malayan Box Turtle

Cuora amboinensis
<u>Size:</u> Up to 8 inches (20 cm). <u>Distribution:</u>
Southeast Asia. <u>Habitat:</u> Shallow lakes and
ponds with shallow shores. These turtles also
spend time on land. <u>Behavior:</u> Active by day.
The Malayan box turtle is a poor swimmer.

An adult snake-necked turtle.

<u>Care:</u> Semiaquatic terrarium with underwater
climbing aids, such as rocks, roots, or sisal rope
ends, so that the turtle can easily reach the
surface of the water. The land portion should
be 30–40 percent of the total area. Water
temperature 75–86°F (24–30°C), air
temperature 79–86°F (26–30°C). <u>Note:</u> If the
temperature drops below 64°F (18°C) for even
a short time, the turtle will become chilled and
can develop a respiratory infection. <u>Diet:</u>
Omnivorous. <u>Hibernation:</u> No. <u>Species requiring
similar conditions:</u> Yellow-margined box turtle,
Cuora flavomarginata. These turtles are from
the Philippines and Sulawesi; this species is
essentially wholly terrestrial. Black marsh turtle,
Siebenrockiella crassicollis. Dwells in shallow
ponds, streams, and rivers; found both in
tropical rain forests and in savannas. Omnivorous
(half meat).

PROFILES:

The painted turtle needs calm waters.

Spiny soft-shell.

Painted Turtle

Chrysemys picta

Size: Up to 10 inches (25 cm). Distribution: Southeast of the Mississippi, and in the north also west of the Mississippi. Habitat: Calm waters, rich in vegetation. Behavior: Active by day; fairly constant alternation between sunning and foraging. Care: Aquarium and garden pond; water temperature 68–77°F (20–25°C), air temperature 68–77°F (20–25°C). In aquarium, provide an overhead spot lamp above an island for warming. Keep in garden pond from June to August. Diet: Omnivorous (half meat). Hibernation: Winter cooling if breeding is desired.

Dandelion greens and blossoms are a favorite for plant-eaters.

Spiny Soft-shell

Trionyx spiniferus

There are 23 species of *Trionyx* worldwide. The two most common are the species from the United States (*Trionyx ferox, Trionyx spiniferus*). Size: Male 6 inches (15 cm), female up to 18 inches (45 cm). Be certain of the species. African soft-shelled turtles can grow to 24 inches (60 cm), and most will readily bite. Distribution: Primarily central and eastern U.S. Habitat: Marshy rivers and streams, lakes. Behavior: Active by day. Care: Aquarium; also in garden pond from June to August. Water temperature 72–81°F (22–27°C), air temperature corresponding to water temperature. Use fine sand in the bottom of the aquarium (river sand, never sharp-grained). The turtle must be able to extend its neck to the surface of the water to breathe when it is dug into the bottom. Diet: Meat (also water snails). Hibernation: Depending on origin; determine by observation. Note: Keep alone. The shell is very sensitive, and injuries heal poorly. The water *must* be clean. A bite from an adult soft-shell can cost a finger. Only for experienced keepers.

Eastern box turtle.

Ornate box turtle.

Terrestrial Turtles

Although these species are in the same group as the basking turtle, they are *wholly* terrestial.

Eastern Box Turtle

Terrapene carolina (4 subspecies)

Size: About 4–8 inches (10–21 cm), depending on subspecies. Distribution: Eastern United States. Habitat: Damp open woodlands and meadows. Behavior: Crepuscular (active in morning and evening twilight). Care: Terrarium and outdoor enclosure; air temperature 64°F (18°C) at night to 82°F (28°C) in the daytime. May be kept outdoors from June to August. Box turtles like early morning and late afternoon sun. Diet: Hunts down and devours earthworms, grasshoppers, crickets, and locusts. Some specimens may eat greens and mushrooms. Hibernation: Yes, depending on area of origin. Special notes: In all but Floridian box turtles, the iris in the male is reddish-brown to orange, while the iris in the female is yellowish-white to yellow (see illustration at right). Box turtles are for experienced keepers only.

A box turtle takes a curious look around.

Ornate Box Turtle

Terrapene ornata

Size: Up to 6 inches (15 cm). Distribution: United States, between the western tributaries of the Mississippi, though not in mountains. Habitat: Grassland; sandy, semidry soil with low bushes, near bodies of water. Hides in burrows. Behavior: Secretive and crepuscular. Care: Terrarium and outdoor enclosure; air temperature 64°F (18°C) at night to 82°F (28°C) in the daytime. Box turtles like early morning and late afternoon sun. Diet: Hunts down and devours earthworms, grasshoppers, crickets, and locusts. Some specimens may eat greens and mushrooms. Hibernation: Yes, even in the first winter. Note: These turtles don't do well in captivity.

PROFILES:

Painted wood turtle.

Vietnamese leaf turtle.

"Land Turtles" That Are Actually Freshwater Turtles

Although the following species are often considered to be land turtles, they are actually semiaquatic. They spend much of their time on land, certainly more than other freshwater turtles, but they also need to live near water.

Painted Wood Turtle

Rhinoclemmys pulcherrima
There are other subspecies as well. Painted wood turtles are often sold in pet shops, and most will do well in the United States. They feed on earthworms, dry dog kibble, and fruit. Shelter: Semiaquatic terrarium with one third water and two thirds land; water temperature 80°F (27°C); air temperature 80–82°F (27–28°C). An overhead spot lamp in one corner of the terrarium provides a warm spot with a temperature of 97°F (36°C). The

terrarium should be covered if needed to keep the humidity at 85–95 percent. Maintain humidity levels to ensure that there is no mildew or mold.

Vietnamese Leaf Turtle
Asian *or* Black-breasted Leaf Turtle
Geoemyda spengleri
Size: Up to 6 inches (15 cm). Distribution: Southern China, Vietnam, Indonesia. Habitat: Rivers and streams in tropical mountain rain forests. Behavior: Active by day. Care: This turtle has a very high mortality rate. Semiaquatic with 50–75 percent land area. Try providing a strong current in the water area. If the turtle seeks it out, keep the current going. A rocky bottom provides good footing. Water temperature 75–79°F (24–26°C), air temperature 75–79°F (24–26°C). The turtle can live in a garden pond with fast-flowing water from June to August. Diet: Mixed. Hibernation: No. Notes: This species has a pronounced hook on its upper jaw, which it uses for climbing. This hook must not be trimmed.

The big-headed turtle often spends the night on land.

Spiny turtle.

Keeled box turtle.

The **big-headed turtle,** *Platysternon megacephalum* (see photograph, page 16), requires an aquarium with shallow water (depth equal to length of the turtle's shell). Water temperatures of 73–75°F (23–24°C); carnivorous. Keep alone. Caution—turtles of this species bite freely.

Spiny Turtle

Heosemys spinosa
<u>Size:</u> Up to 8.5 inches (22 cm). <u>Distribution:</u> Thailand, Malayan peninsula, Sumatra, Borneo. <u>Habitat:</u> Mountain streams of tropical rain forests. <u>Behavior:</u> Active by day. <u>Care:</u> Aquaterrarium with 40–50 percent land area; water temperature 75–79°F (24–26°C). Likes fast-flowing, shallow water with secure footing (stones and roots). <u>Diet:</u> Mixed. <u>Hibernation:</u> No. <u>Note:</u> This turtle has a high mortality rate in the United States. It is rarely available.

Keeled Box Turtle

Pyxidea mouhoti
<u>Size:</u> Up to 7 inches (18 cm). <u>Distribution:</u> Vietnam, Laos. <u>Habitat:</u> In and around waters of the tropical rain forest. <u>Behavior:</u> Juveniles are semiaquatic, whereas older turtles are mainly terrestrial. They burrow in the moist, leafy forest floor and enjoy the green shade. <u>Care:</u> Semiaquatic tank; water temperature 73–77°F (23–25°C), air temperature 73–77°F (23–25°C), soil temperature 68–72°F (20–22°C). <u>Diet:</u> Omnivorous. <u>Hibernation:</u> No. <u>Note:</u> This turtle has a high mortality rate in the United States. This species of turtle has a pronounced hook on its upper jaw, which it uses for climbing.

Lean beef, ground or minced, makes good food for freshwater turtles.

Species Conservation

The Washington Convention on International Trade in Endangered Species of Wild Fauna and Flora (CITES) protects flora and fauna whose worldwide survival is threatened. Depending on how much protection is needed, various species of turtles are listed in categories I or II. Animals threatened with extinction are listed in Appendix I. These animals may not be sold or bought without special permission. Other turtles are listed under CITES in Appendix II. Being placed on one of the CITES appendices only means that special permits are needed before the animals can be imported into the United States; CITES does not affect the sale or transport of animals within the United States.

Many states protect their native turtles, forbidding harassment or removal from the wild and prohibiting private possession, commercial trade, or barter in the protected species. The Federal Endangered Species Act enforces state protection by prohibiting (without a permit) interstate transport, trade, or barter in any protected species. In addition, public health laws in the United States prohibit the sale or trade of any turtles under 3 inches (7.5 cm) in length, except for scientific purposes.

Be aware that individual states may change their regulations for individual species of turtles from time to time.

Stay dated on current regulations and laws by inquiring at your local state game and fish agency or at the game and fish agency of the state in question. It is your responsibility to check with the appropriate authorities to be sure your purchase is legal.

Where to Buy a Turtle

A pet shop: You don't have to worry about buying a turtle from a reputable pet shop. Your receipt, with the scientific name of the turtle, will serve as your turtle's "papers." Never buy a turtle on the spur of the moment. Ask for the turtle's scientific name, and find out what sort of care it requires before you buy (ask the pet shop staff or a turtle expert, or consult the profiles in this book).

Turtles from species that are not protected are occasionally offered for sale, but some, like the ornate box turtle (see page 15), may not do well in captivity. Furthermore, many species become quite large; others, like the soft-shelled turtles and snapping turtles, are suitable only for solitary living quarters.

A breeder: Thanks to successful breeding practices, it is no longer difficult to buy a captive bred turtle of a CITES-protected species.

Breeders often advertise in magazines for terrarium and aquarium owners as well as in the specialized turtle and reptile publications (see Information, page 62). It's best to visit the breeder to see how the turtles are cared for, where they are kept, and what their winter quarters look like. You can ask the breeder to show you his breeding stock, and maybe even your turtle's parents.

Colorful companion: the red-bellied short-necked turtle (Emydura albertisii).

Checklist for a Healthy Turtle

What to look for	Semiaquatic and Aquatic Turtles
Shell in good condition	*Young turtles:* Up to one third of adult size: Firm and elastic shell, like a thumbnail. *Adult turtles:* Hard and firm shell. All scutes (horny plates) firm and intact (check the underside as well). Algae growth is acceptable. Note: Semiaquatic and snake-necked turtles regularly shed the colorless outer layer.
Shell in poor condition	*Young turtles and adults:* Shell gives way when pressed, like crust on a dinner roll (soft, not elastic). *Adults:* Firm, but then changes shape. Individual plates very bumpy, or profile from the side as very bumpy. *Plastron:* Holes in horny plate; pink, watery blisters under or in horny plate; loose or missing plates, bare (whitish-yellow) bone exposed.
Skin healthy	Outside of heavy scales on neck and legs, skin is leathery, soft, and elastic.
Skin not healthy	Cracked. Terrestrial: Infested with ticks and mites.
Eyes healthy	Clear, bright, opened wide.
Eyes not healthy	Cornea clouded, lids closed, swollen.
Nose healthy	Dry, no bubbles, no noise when breathing.
Respiratory tract not healthy	Bubbles at nose and mouth, opens mouth wide while craning the neck, rattle when breathing.
Claws healthy	Firmly attached to foot, with healthy nail bed; no missing claws.
Claws not healthy	Claws loosely embedded or missing; nail bed inflamed (reddish or whitish) and/or swollen.
Movement	*On land:* All four legs used for forward motion; no dragging of rear legs (nerve damage!). *In water:* When viewed from the front, does not tilt to one side when swimming (lung damage!).
General responsiveness	When picked up, the turtle either moves vigorously in defense or pulls back strongly into its shell.

When held like this, a healthy turtle makes defensive motions.

A reputable breeder will also serve as a knowledgeable resource if you have any questions or problems later.

Note: If you can't find the turtle you want at a pet shop, you may be able to order one from the breeder. While you wait for your turtle to be hatched, you'll have time to prepare suitable living quarters and learn how to take care of your future pet. Be sure to purchase the right kind of terrarium and other accessories for the type of turtle you are acquiring (see pages 21–29).

When to Get a Turtle

Species that hibernate (see Profiles, pages 10–17) are best purchased in the summertime—not earlier than May or later than September. In the autumn, you may have difficulty determining whether an unresponsive turtle is about to hibernate or is ill. If you have actually purchased a sick turtle and place it in hibernation, it will most likely die before springtime.

It's also not advisable to buy a turtle that is just coming out of hibernation. If it had the beginnings of a health problem at the start of winter, the problem will not become apparent for 4–8 weeks after the turtle awakens.

Species from semitropical and tropical regions do not hibernate. These turtles are, however, very sensitive to drafts. These species must be kept absolutely warm and secure when they are moved in winter (see HOW-TO, page 30). **Note:** Use the table on page 19 to check the turtle's health before you make your decision.

Determining a Turtle's Age

Some turtles are known to have lived for more than 100 years. However, the age of a turtle can be determined with relative reliability only when the turtle is young. If you know the turtle's eventual adult size (see Profiles, pages 10–17), and if your turtle is approximately one third this large, it is about three years old. After another three years, it will have reached two thirds of its adult size. Be aware that this is only a rough rule of thumb, because how fast a turtle grows depends a great deal on its living conditions. Furthermore, the growth rate slows as the turtle gets older.

Note: You cannot tell a turtle's age by counting the growth rings on the plates of its shell.

Proper Shelter

The species you choose will determine the type of living quarters your pet turtle needs—either a terrarium or an aquarium, along with the appropriate technical equipment (see "Important Note," page 63). Outdoors, the sun provides the natural light and warmth essential for your turtle's health; indoors, you must supply these by artificial measures. The size and layout of the terrarium or aquarium will also make a difference in how comfortably your turtle settles into its home.

Terrarium for Semiaquatic Turtles

In addition to a land area with interesting variety, semiaquatic turtles need a sizeable pool of water for swimming and diving (see drawing, page 24). Therefore, the terrarium should

Yellow-bellied slider baby. The shell colors will fade as the turtle gets older.

definitely be water-tight; it's a good idea to buy an aquarium right from the start.
It's important to know what your particular turtle requires.

A good swimmer needs plenty of room to swim. A turtle that climbs around under water must have objects to provide secure footing, such as submerged rocks, roots, and sisal rope ends. For a semiaquatic turtle that spends most of its time on land, the land area must take up at least half the space.

The terrarium size for a single semiaquatic turtle can be calculated as follows: The shell length of the adult turtle (see Profiles, pages 10–17), multiplied by five, gives the length and width of the terrarium base. Increase this area by 30 percent for each additional turtle.
Note: The larger the area, the happier the turtle will be. Also, it's easier to provide an interesting layout in a large terrarium.

In temperate areas, the land and water areas may need to be heated.

✔ The following system (see drawing, page 24) will provide the necessary warmth: First, place a sheet of pressed cork, .5–1 inch (1–2 cm) thick, on the floor of the terrarium to cover one half to one third of its area. On top of this, place three layers of aluminum foil, shiny side up. On the aluminum foil, place a tank heating pad with a thermostat (available at pet shops), about the same size as the foil area.

✔ Now set a water basin made of clay, porcelain, or metal on the heating mat, leaving room to place flat rocks around the edge. These will help keep the water clean; when heated from below, they also provide a basking spot.
Note: Depending on your turtle's needs, the water area should take up one third to one half of the total space. Construct the pool so that the turtle can glide slowly into the water. At its deepest point, the water should be a little deeper than the width of the turtle's shell. Otherwise, if the turtle falls on its back, it may be unable to right itself in the shallow water, and it can drown.

✔ Now cover the terrarium floor with a half-and-half mixture of fine-grained, washed river sand and bark chips.

✔ Arrange roots and rocks in such a way that the turtle must climb over or around them. Also give your turtle a place to hide.

✔ An overhead spot lamp (60–100 watts, depending on its distance from the turtle) serves as a heat source for basking.

✔ For overall daytime illumination, you can install a fluorescent tube above the terrarium.

✔ An ultraviolet lamp or a full-spectrum light (Vita-Lite by Duro-Test) is needed if you intend to raise young turtles or if you aren't able to move your pets outdoors in the summer.
Note: Electrically heated rocks (available at pet shops) are another option for local warmth. Monitor the rock's temperature; malfunctioning rocks can burn your pet.

The common musk turtle is a poor swimmer and needs secure footing even underwater.

Place the light about 1 foot (30 cm) above the terrarium and turn it on at noontime every day for about 15–30 minutes.

Note: Don't install the overhead spot lamp or other light so that it shines through a pane of glass; the heat may cause the glass to shatter. A timer for the lighting is a convenient option.

✔ Your turtles may eat any plants inside the terrarium. Plan on replacing the plants or put them around the outside. If the terrarium is in a dark spot, you will need to install a special plant lamp (available in florist or pet shops) to keep the plants healthy.

The Australian snake-necked turtle returns the photographer's attention with an alert gaze.

Aquarium for Aquatic Turtles

First, determine whether your aquatic turtle is a good or poor swimmer (see Profiles, pages 10–17). Energetic swimmers want as much swimming space as possible. For that reason, the surface area and depth of the aquarium are important. The water should be at least 1 foot (30 cm) deep, but in any case deeper than the width of your turtle's shell. Otherwise, if it lands on its back, it may drown. A depth of about 18 inches (45 cm) is comfortable.

The minimum size of an aquarium for one turtle is calculated as follows: The length should equal five times the shell length of the adult turtle.

The width is three times the shell length. This calculation does not include any space for decorations. Therefore, increase the calculated aquarium volume by about 30 percent. Add another 30 percent if you want to keep two turtles in the same aquarium.

Setting up the aquarium is simple if you are content with the minimum of equipment.

✔ Cover the glass bottom with a thin layer of washed sand, so that it won't act as a mirror. You can substitute river rock pellets if you prefer; but your turtle may find the pebbles too heavy for burrowing.

✔ A piece of ridge tile on the aquarium floor provides a hiding place; a branch of resinous wood from a bog will give the turtle something to climb on underwater and to bask on above the surface. **Note:** The basking island must always be firmly anchored and must not wobble or tip over when the turtle climbs on it. Unanchored corkboard will not do!

✔ Gather flat stones, and build a wall at the rear of the aquarium to provide an attractive setting. This also gives poor swimmers a way to clamber out of the water. Polyurethane foam glue or ready-mix cement helps keep the stones in place. Leave a narrow space of about 1–2 inches (3–5 cm) between the stones and the rear wall. This will later allow you to insert a tube to suction out the dirt that settles there. It works best to place a Styrofoam block against the rear of the aquarium before you build the stone wall and then remove it when the wall is complete.

An attractive home for a semiaquatic turtle, with a generous swimming basin.

Pressed corkboards, aluminum foil, and a heating mat provide heat from below.

Water basin.

Heating pad.

Three layers of aluminum foil.

Corkboard.

Mixture of sand and bark.

Caution: Young turtles could get stuck in this crevice and drown. Close the gap with a strip of Styrofoam; remove it for cleaning.

✔ The most convenient way to simultaneously heat and filter the aquarium water is to use a pump-driven filter which contains a thermostat-controlled heating unit (available in pet shops). When choosing a filter, consider whether your turtle prefers calm or moving water (see Profiles, pages 10–17). This will determine the necessary pump output. The more water the pump puts out per minute, the stronger the water flow and turbulence in the aquarium.

✔ Basking spots must lie just below and at the surface of the water, and they must not give way or wobble as the turtle climbs on them. Take two pieces of corkboard about .5 inch (1 cm) thick, and glue each one to a piece of plexiglass with epoxy glue. Fasten the two together at all four corners with very strong wire to make a two-story structure. The wire must be stiff, so the island won't wobble. Suspend the structure from the edge or a crosspiece of the aquarium frame. Slabs of slate or cement are more durable than cork, but also "colder." The lower level should rest horizontally under the surface, just deep enough that the turtle can crane its neck and breathe. The upper level, set off to one side if possible, should be slanted so the turtle can easily crawl up onto it.

*Aquarium
for an aquatic
turtle, with rock wall
and an island for sunning.*

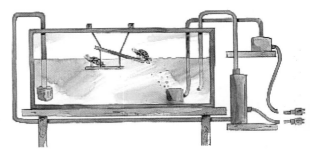

*Technical equipment: an aquarium filter with
integrated heating element and air pump.*

✔ A glass lid protects against drafts. Install the lid in such a way that there is an opening in the middle, above the sunning island.
✔ Above this opening, hang an overhead spot lamp and a full-spectrum lamp (Vita-Lite by Duro-Test), and perhaps a fluorescent tube for general illumination of the aquarium (see page 22).

Where to Put the Terrarium or Aquarium

The site you choose for your turtle's home must meet certain criteria.

It should be bright. The ideal location is under a glass roof, such as in a greenhouse. Natural light enters from above, and the turtle experiences the changing day lengths during the different seasons. This has an important influence on its readiness for hibernation or breeding. Rooms with large windows are also very suitable. In dark rooms, you must provide adequate artificial lighting to simulate daylight and seasonal variations.

It must be quiet. Turtles are easily disturbed by noise and will not thrive near the television, for example. Do not let vibrations from a refrigerator, stereo equipment, or the aquarium pump rattle your terrarium or aquarium.

It must be protected from drafts. Drafts are harmful for all turtles. Never place a terrarium or aquarium directly by a window or on the floor.

Outdoor Enclosures

Turtles that don't get enough light, sunshine, and vitamins can develop metabolic bone disease (MBD) (rickets). Both the shell and bones become soft. Many semiaquatic and aquatic turtles will benefit from living outdoors from June to August, even in more northern latitudes. If you provide a cold frame with an additional heat source, your turtle can enjoy fresh outdoor air from May to September.

Designing the outdoor pool: A bigger pond is easier to maintain. The pond should hold at least 80 gallons of water (about 300 liters). You can use a readymade garden pond, purchased at a garden shop. When properly installed, this provides secure footing and a watertight pool. For larger ponds, you might also consider a plastic liner; follow the manufacturer's instructions for installation.

The protected wood turtle is a good pet for those experienced in turtle care.

Basking log: Place a thick log in the pond so that the turtle can easily climb on it for sunning. Should danger threaten, the turtle can quickly drop into the water.

Vegetation: The most suitable choices are reeds and cattails. Anything else will be eaten, as will small fish, newts, and insect larvae.

Filtering: Pools with a capacity of up to 50 cubic feet (1.5 cubic meters) must be filtered; filtering is optional for larger ponds. Install a simple submersible pump at the bottom of the pool and an external pool filter nearby (both are available in garden and pet shops; follow the manufacturer's instructions). The filtered water will flow back into the pool. If you have space, you can direct the flow through a small running stream. Turtles that enjoy fast-flowing water will gravitate toward this brooklet.

Installation: A readymade pond should be installed at a slight angle. Excess water—for instance, after a downpour—will then run off at the lower edge. Use the runoff to water your garden, or construct a small drainage ditch. A pond with a plastic liner should have a slight hollow at a suitable spot on the upper edge to serve as a runoff basin.

Fencing: The pond area must be enclosed securely enough that the turtle cannot escape. An attractive option consists of planks, planed smooth and treated with a preservative; these can be set into the ground in a pleasing shape, not necessarily a rectangle or square. Also suitable are lawn-edging tiles made of concrete, metal, or corrugated plastic (found in garden shops). To determine the height, consider that an adult turtle must not be able to reach the top edge with its front feet when standing on its hind legs. A fence that rises 1.5–2 feet high (50–60 cm) will usually suffice. The fencing must also extend about 1 foot (20–30 cm) into the ground; otherwise, the turtle may dig its way out.

TIP

Recapturing Your Outdoor Pet

Many freshwater turtles retain their wild ways; if they have enjoyed the freedom of a large garden pond, they may be difficult to catch at the end of the outdoor season. Therefore, it's a good idea to establish a regular feeding spot along the shore. When the time comes to bring your turtle indoors, spread a piece of fishnet or bird netting under the feeding spot, covering an area of about one square yard (1 m²). Camouflage it with a thin layer of sand. Tie stout cords to the four corners and extend them a good distance away from the pond, two in each direction. With a partner, wait for your pet to approach the feeding spot. Pull on the cords to trap the turtle in the net, then use the net to carry your pet securely to its indoor living quarters.

A chainlink fence is not a good choice, because some turtles will climb it and because babies crawl through it. Also, any large branches or rocks should be far enough from the fence that they won't provide an escape route. **Note:** Young turtles, or any smaller than 4 inches (10 cm) long, are easy prey for jays, crows, raccoons, and—near the seacoast—gulls. For protection, cover the enclosure with bird netting or a fishnet.

Cold frame: In temperate areas, you can install a cold frame made of plexiglass in your pond. Because of the greenhouse effect, this will hold sufficient warmth even in relatively long periods of bad weather. The shelter should not have a floor; if you place it with the doorway end partially immersed in the water, the turtle will be able to swim right up into a warm and protected space. For cold days, when the temperature in the shelter doesn't reach 79°F (26°C), install an infrared lamp, or a 60- to 80-watt light bulb, that can hang from the ceiling. **Note:** Cold frame kits can be purchased in garden shops. A glazier will have to cut the plexiglass pieces. These are easily inserted into the frame kit.

Fresh Summer Air on Balcony or Patio

Even if you don't have a yard or garden, your turtle can still enjoy the outdoors. All you need is a balcony or patio that receives at least two hours of direct sunlight daily and is protected from the wind (see drawings on page 29). This can be your turtle's home from early May to September. The pen should be large enough to provide shade if the sun is too hot.

✔ First, build a box from squared timbers and spruce boards, about 5–6 feet (1.6–2 m) long, 2 feet (60 cm) wide, and 2.5–3 feet (80–100 cm) high (about as high as the windowsill or balcony railing). To keep the box from rotting, line it with a plastic sheet, fastened at the edges with waterproof adhesive.

A cold frame with a heat source extends the outdoor season.

This outdoor pen offers freshwater turtles a natural diversity of terrain.

place beneath them. Then pass rubber cords (about $^3/_{16}$ inch or 5 mm) through holes drilled in the plexiglass panes and fasten them to hooks on the front of the box.

✔ Fill the bottom of the box 4 inches (10 cm) deep with pumice rock. On this, place the pool; depending on the number of turtles, use one or two mortar pans from a hardware store, or a readymade pool. Be sure the top of the pool is at least 12 inches (30 cm) below the edge of the box, so the turtle can't climb out.

✔ Now add another 8–12 inches (20–30 cm) of pumice.

✔ Fill the box with garden soil to the edge of the pool.

✔ Add plants and decorations to your landscape to suit your own taste.

✔ Secure your balcony so the turtle can't fall off if it should escape the pen.

Turtles in their summer quarters on a sunny balcony.

✔ For a cover on colder days, use two plexiglass panes about 3 feet (1 m) wide, screwed to a frame made of roofing laths. When not in use, the cover stows easily behind the box.

✔ Have the cover extend a little over the front edge (for rain protection). The box should be about 4–6 inches (10–15 cm) lower in front than in back, so that the plexiglass panes lie at an angle. This allows more sunlight to enter, and the rain can run off better.

✔ Monitor the temperature with a thermometer at all times. The temperature should meet the range given for your turtle's species (see Profiles, pages 10–17); you can raise the lid with blocks of wood or remove it.

✔ To secure the cover against storms, attach metal angles (with predrilled holes) at the back of the box so that the cover just slides into

Metal angles, rubber cords, and hooks secure the pen's cover against severe storms.

Transporting a Turtle

Freshwater turtles are extremely sensitive to cold and drafts. If you must transport a turtle during cold weather, be very careful. Fill a hot-water bottle with warm water [about 86°F (30°C)] and place it in a cardboard box (a shoebox is fine). Put your turtle in a pillow-case or cotton bag (turned inside out), and tie the sack closed. Now place the turtle on the hot-water bottle. Close the box and wrap it in a wool blanket. This will protect your turtle for about one hour of cold outdoor travel.

A warm traveling box is essential, especially in winter. Even a few breaths of ice-cold air can lead to serious illness.

Quarantine Is Important

When you bring a newly acquired turtle home, you should first put it in quarantine. It might have a worm infestation or a bacterial, viral, or amoebic infection. You can't tell just by looking at it; you must have a stool sample analyzed (see top of page 31). The turtle will remain in quarantine until it is officially declared to be healthy.

Before putting the turtle in quarantine, give it a good bath. For a semiaquatic turtle, use a good-sized bowl of warm water [79°F (26°C)], not too deep. Be sure the turtle can easily hold its head above water; let it paddle about for 10–20 minutes. Aquatic turtles should also have a bath before being placed in the quarantine aquarium; this will help keep the water clean much longer. Once a veterinarian has performed a stool analysis and declares your newly acquired turtle healthy, you can place it in the terrarium with your other turtles.

Quarantine terrarium for semiaquatic turtles. It can be made of glass or plastic and contains only the bare essentials.

Taking Stool Samples

Stool samples are analyzed by a veterinarian.

Veterinarians can supply containers for stool specimens.

You will need three containers; some are made for this purpose, but empty film canisters will do. Take a stool sample every day for three days. Add a drop of water to each container so the sample will not dry out and lose its value for testing. The oldest sample must be no more than five days old when it is submitted for analysis. Until then, keep the stool samples in the refrigerator to prevent the growth of mold.

A simple quarantine aquarium for aquatic turtles. A piece of ridge tile provides a hiding place.

Quarantine Quarters

Because cleanliness is important, the quarantine terrarium or aquarium must be simple, even spartan. Dirty corners and crannies are breeding grounds for pathogens and worm eggs.

For semiaquatic turtles, a simple aquarium made of glass makes a good quarantine terrarium. It needs only a water basin of suitable size and a food dish. A board resting on two bricks provides a hiding place. Two wooden ramps permit the turtle to climb around and to gain access to the bathing pool (see drawing, page 30).

For aquatic turtles, the quarantine aquarium is equally spartan. Simply set a piece of

ridge tile down to provide a hiding place. The basking island described on page 25 provides a resting spot. Of course, the quarantine aquarium also needs the basic technical equipment (see pages 23–26).

Note: A black plastic mortar pan (from the hardware store) with a capacity of 12–65 gallons (about 50–250 liters) can also serve as quarantine quarters. Use the same basic equipment as in a glass aquarium.

A mortar pan like this can even be used as hibernation quarters in winter (see page 36).

PROPER CARE AND FEEDING

Allow your turtle to hibernate if necessary. Supply a varied diet of healthy foods. Provide suitable conditions for breeding, if that is your plan. Don't hesitate to take a sick turtle to the veterinarian. If you follow these simple rules, you and your pet turtle will enjoy many years together.

Housing Turtles Together

If you have no experience in turtle care, you may want to start with just one, to lessen the work involved. If you want to give your turtle a companion, here are things to keep in mind:

✔ It's essential to provide one or two more sunning spots and hideaways than there are turtles in the terrarium or aquarium.

✔ A long-established inhabitant will vigorously defend its territory—that is, the entire terrarium or aquarium—against a newcomer. If this happens, the old-timer should be sent to quarantine quarters (see page 31) for about two weeks. During that time, the newly acquired turtle can explore the territory, gain confidence, and become less readily intimidated.

✔ If the turtles continue to do battle despite all your precautions or if one tends to stay in hiding and even refuses to eat, you will have no choice but to separate them permanently.

The common musk turtle likes to climb around underwater. Provide roots, rocks, or other climbing aids.

Hibernation Can Be Important

In the wild, turtles living in regions where winter is cold and food is scarce survive these hostile conditions by going into hibernation. But not all turtles that hibernate in the wild need to hibernate in captivity, even to reproduce.

During this winter rest, all their metabolic processes are reduced. Their heart rate and breathing slow down; they move hardly at all. In this state, living off their small reserves of fat, they are able to stay alive through the usually short winters of their native habitats.

If you have a turtle of hibernating species, provide a winter resting period if not hibernation. This will have a positive effect on the reproductive behavior of adult turtles.

Natural hibernation: If you live in a temperate area and keep your turtles outdoors, Eastern, Three-toed, Ornate, and Desert Box turtles are likely candidates for natural hibernation. These turtles naturally hibernate on land and are very adept at finding suitable spots for hibernating in captivity. Make sure that they dig below the frost line and that they have not dug into a flood prone area.

Artificial hibernation: Artificial hibernation may be arranged in several ways. If you live in

—————————— **T I P** ——————————

What If It Wakes Up Too Soon?

One day you may check on your hibernating turtle, only to find that it has already emerged and is swimming around with a lively air. If this happens, first weigh it; if your pet has lost more than 10% of its weight, take it to the veterinarian. Otherwise, follow the steps described on page 37 to return the turtle to its regular living quarters (see pages 21–26). If it begins to eat again within the expected time, it is probably healthy. Move the hibernation quarters to a warm room [72°F (22°C)] and wait until the water has reached room temperature. Then place the turtle back in its terrarium with water at the same temperature. Turn on the heating and lighting systems, and gradually increase the temperature.

a mild climate, use of a modified refrigerator is a preferred method. Place each aquatic and semiterrestrial turtle in an individual plastic box filled with moist, unmilled sphagnum moss. Store the boxes in a refrigerator modified to retain temperatures between 40 and 44°F (4.4–6.6°C). Check each turtle periodically.

The length of your turtle's hibernation period depends on the native habitat of its particular species. You will need to do a little research. When the average daytime temperatures in your turtle's homeland stay below about 62–64°F (17–18°C), it is time for your pet to hibernate. When the temperatures rise and remain above this temperature, the hibernation period is over. As a rule, the normal hibernation period for a turtle is four to six months.

Note: Young turtles should not be allowed to hibernate longer than two to three months. If necessary, wake them up (see page 37).

Signs That Your Turtle Is Ready to Hibernate

With experience, even a novice turtle owner can learn to recognize a turtle's readiness for hibernation. In October, as the length of the day and the strength of the sun decrease, turtles become more sluggish and have little appetite. They spend less time swimming about and more time lazing with their heads poked into the darkest corner of their shelter. When this happens, even if some days are still warm, stop feeding your pet. A turtle needs about one week to digest the food it has already eaten and completely empty its bowels before it hibernates.

A turtle that is sick must be taken to the veterinarian and restored to good health before being allowed to hibernate.

Note: For detailed instructions for overwintering your turtle, please turn to pages 36–37.

What If Your Turtle Won't Hibernate?

Even if your turtle is older and hasn't been overwintered in years, it may be able to hibernate. Follow the steps described on page 36. If you have turned off the heating and lighting systems in the terrarium or aquarium and your turtle doesn't respond right away with diminishing activity and appetite, don't be concerned. Go ahead and put it in the hibernation quarters you have prepared (see pages 36–37). Wait for a week. If it has not yet settled into hibernation, observe it carefully and weigh it more often. If your pet loses 10% of its body weight within two to three weeks, it is not strong enough to hibernate, and you must take it to the veterinarian. A healthy turtle will go into hibernation within two to three weeks even if it has not hibernated in years.

Ten Golden Rules
for a Healthy Turtle

1 Be aware that turtles of different species have different needs (see Profiles, pages 10–17), and ensure that they are met.

2 If your turtle is of a species that hibernates, it may or may not need to in captivity.

3 Four weeks before you start to hibernate your turtle, carefully evaluate its health and have stool samples tested for worms. A turtle that isn't healthy might not survive the hibernation period.

4 Don't expose your turtle to drafts. Drafts cause illnesses that can be fatal.

5 Be sure the water in the aquarium or the terrarium pool is always clean. Otherwise, bacteria and viruses can multiply and make your turtle sick.

6 Give your turtle a varied diet of healthy foods that contain the nutrients it needs (see page 38).

7 Supply vitamins carefully. An excess of vitamins can lead to serious health problems (see page 51).

8 Do not keep too many turtles in one aquarium. The water quality can deteriorate rapidly, and your turtles will not thrive.

9 If two or more turtles do not get along, you must separate them permanently. Constant scuffling causes stress and lowers disease resistance.

10 Adequate ultraviolet light is essential. If your turtle doesn't get natural sunlight outdoors, you must provide the appropriate conditions in the indoor terrarium or aquarium (see pages 21–26).

Turtle Grooming

Trimming the claws: A freshwater turtle's claws may grow too long only if it walks around too little or if the ground underfoot is too soft. If the claws do not wear down as they should, they must be trimmed. It's best to have your veterinarian teach you how to trim the claws.

Note: The males of some freshwater turtles, such as the painted turtle, have longer claws on their front feet (see profiles, pages 10–17). These must not be trimmed. They are a natural sex characteristic and are important for courtship (see page 43). Rarely, the horny beak around the mouth may grow to be too long if the turtle's food is too soft. The horny excess must be filed off by a veterinarian. However, the painted wood turtle, for example, naturally has a hook on its upper jaw, which aids it in climbing. This must never be trimmed.

Grooming Tools

It's a good idea to purchase a few simple grooming tools. For example, a disposable syringe (without a needle) is useful for administering liquid medications.

Disposable syringe (without needle) for administering liquid medications.

Overwintering a Freshwater Turtle

✔ Well before hibernation, if there is any doubt that your turtle is healthy, consult a veterinarian and have stool samples analyzed (see page 31).

✔ It's not necessary to bathe the turtle to help it completely empty its bowels. However, copious bowel movements in the fall are a sign that your turtle is preparing to hibernate.

✔ Turn off the heat and light in the terrarium or aquarium. The filter and air pump can stay on.

✔ Wait until the water cools to room temperature. Keep the water temperature below 64°F (18°C) for a few days.

✔ When the turtle becomes relatively sluggish and stops eating, place it in its hibernation quarters.

A plastic mortar pan makes ideal winter quarters for a freshwater turtle.

The claws are neatly trimmed with special clippers sold in pet stores.

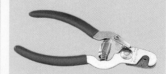

Special clippers for trimming the claws.

Freshwater turtles will encounter ticks only if kept outdoors. These parasites can be removed easily with special tick pullers.

Tick pullers. Available from outdoor suppliers.

The *vegetable bin of your refrigerator can serve as hibernation quarters if a suitable cellar is not available. A loose layer of sphagnum moss creates an artificial mud-bottom.*

Care of Shelter

Semiaquatic turtles: Remove feces and urine from terrarium every day. Scrub the bathing pool and change the water.

Aquatic turtles: Change water daily in a small aquarium, weekly in a large aquarium.

Hibernation Quarters

In the wild, most freshwater turtles that hibernate choose the muddy bottom of a pond, river, or other body of water. Pet turtles can hibernate in a black plastic mortar pan (see drawing, page 36).

Shelter for a smaller turtle can be provided by a ridge tile set on the bottom of the pan; for larger turtles, create a cave effect by covering part of the pan with a board to block out light.

The water level should be shallow enough that a turtle sitting on the bottom can breathe by craning its neck.

The water temperature can vary between 34°F and 54°F (1–12°C); if it stays above 54°F (12°C) for long, the turtle will awaken too soon.

Change the water every three to four weeks. Change the water immediately if it turns yellowish or if a whitish film forms on the water.

Note: Aeration and filtering are not necessary in the hibernation quarters. The turtle must not be fed while hibernating.

A refrigerator can provide emergency hibernation quarters for your freshwater turtle if a suitable cellar location is not available (see drawing at left). Cover the glass plate above the vegetable bin with foil to block the light. You don't need to provide a special hiding place.

The water level should be the same as in the mortar pan.

Note: See if your turtle will accept an artificial mud-bottom. Fill the bottom of the mortar pan or vegetable bin with a loose layer of sphagnum moss. This gives the turtle the feeling of security.

How a Turtle Wakes Up

Your turtle will emerge from hibernation after three to four months, depending on the length of winter in its natural habitat. When it does, move the hibernation quarters to a warm room [72°F (22°C)], and wait until the water has reached room temperature. Then put the turtle back in the semiaquatic terrarium or aquarium, with water at the same temperature. Turn on the heating and lighting systems again. Increase the temperature gradually over several days. After two to seven days, the turtle will resume its normal level of activity and begin to eat again.

VACATION CARE

Plan ahead to find a reliable person to care for your turtle in its familiar surroundings.
Checklist for Vacation Care
✔ Equipment: Explain how to recognize if something is wrong. Show how to perform a simple inspection and what to do for simple repairs. Provide the name and address of a knowledgeable person who can help. Demonstrate procedures for routine care (such as cleaning filters). Have replacement bulbs on hand. In the fuse box, identify the circuit breaker for the electrical equipment.
✔ Feeding: Write down how much and what to feed. Specify how often and when to feed.
✔ Turtle care: Describe normal behavior. Point out any peculiarities of behavior. Is it almost mating season, or time for the turtle to lay eggs? (See pages 42–44.) Is the turtle just coming out of hibernation? Describe possible illnesses (see pages 48–51).
Be sure to leave your vacation address, and the telephone numbers of your veterinarian and an expert who can be called on for advice.

A Healthy Diet

If your turtle had its way, every meal would consist of bits of trout or crabmeat. However, such a diet is too lopsided. Your pet would get fat without getting the nutrients it needs to stay fit. Instead, give your turtle a variety of healthy foods from the start.

The Right Food

Freshwater turtles are omnivores; they eat both plants and animals. In general, however, most species prefer meat (see Profiles, pages 10–17).

Suitable dietary staples for these turtles include fat-free ground beef, small aquarium fish (guppies), or bits of filleted freshwater fish, such as trout. They will also relish water snails, which you can breed in a small aquarium (starter kits are available at pet shops). If you are away from home for a long time, your turtle-sitter will find it convenient to feed your turtle commercial floating turtle food. In a pinch, use cat chow. Unfortunately, the dry cat chow also contains fats that are difficult to digest; therefore, although this can be a basic food, it should never be given as the only food. **Note:** If the dry food causes diarrhea, stop giving it until your turtle's digestive system returns to normal. Then give it in smaller amounts.

Plants in the diet include tender herbs such as parsley, lemon balm, or basil; well-washed greens (romaine or escarole, dandelions, clover, Chinese cabbage, chard, collards, endive); vegetables such as green beans, chopped tomatoes, celery, cauliflower, beet greens, broccoli, carrots; and fruits such as pears, apples, blackberries, blueberries, cantaloupe, strawberries, raspberries, or bananas.

A plump earthworm makes a tasty treat for this eastern box turtle.

Dietary Supplements

Minerals and trace elements are essential for a turtle's healthy development. These are found in commercial diet supplements, such as ReptaMin or Osteoform, which are generally sold as powders. Every turtle needs one pinch of this powder twice a week. Mix it thoroughly with your turtle's favorite food.

Calcium is important for shell development in growing turtles and for the formation of eggshells in adult females. Calcium is available as a special preparation in pet shops, or you can meet your turtle's needs by adding ground eggshells to the diet.

Note: Bananas, tomatoes, and peaches are high in phosphorus. Too much phosphorus, like too little calcium, can cause MBD (rickets), which weakens the turtle's shell. A good balance of calcium to phosphorus in a turtle's diet is 3:1 to 5:1. When you offer phosphorus-rich foods such as tomatoes, add a little calcium to compensate.

Vitamin supplements are usually not needed if a turtle is eating fresh ground beef or fish, or while it is kept outdoors in the summer months.

A Healthy Diet for Turtles

Who?	How often?	How much?	What else:
Freshwater turtles (young)	Daily, one or two times	Daily ration: half the maximum amount that the turtle can eat at one time (see checklist, page 41).	Healthy bone growth requires regular feeding of calcium, mineral salt mixtures, and vitamin-rich food (see page 39).
Freshwater turtles (juvenile/adult)	Every other day; for adults, alternating two- and three-day intervals.	Half the amount that the turtle can eat in one meal before it is completely full (see checklist, page 41).	An egg-laying female needs extra calcium to build the egg shells. Give calcium supplements in the form of crushed eggshells (1/5 of a normal hen's egg daily) for four weeks before and four weeks after she lays her eggs.

Golden rule for feeding: The only way to determine whether your turtle is getting the right amount of food is to weigh it regularly. Weigh young turtles every three to four weeks (use a postage scale); weigh adult turtles every four to six weeks. The turtle should be gaining weight. Weight gain is proportionately greater in young turtles than in older turtles.

Note: If your turtle loses weight (except after laying eggs and during hibernation), either your pet is sick or you must increase its daily food ration.

Because the body can produce vitamin A, it should be necessary only to provide foods high in carotene. Pet shops offer special fish food called Koi-Chow, which also gives the turtle's skin a splendid color and makes the yellow or red spots and stripes stand out beautifully. Spinach and carrots are also rich in carotene; you can feed these instead of aquatic plants.

Note: An excess of vitamins can cause severe health problems in turtles (see page 51).

Male North American wood turtles are feisty and aggressive toward other males.

Make Your Own Special Turtle Food

The recipe below is a practical way to keep turtle food on hand. This complete turtle food can be made in bulk and frozen in portions for later use.

Basic formula for carnivorous (aquatic) turtles: 75% animal protein, of the following composition: 30% freshwater fish, 30% heart (for example, beef heart), 20% cuttlefish, 20% liver. Chicken eggs or shrimp (both with shells) can be used to change the flavor or composition of the food. The remaining 25% of the total is a combination of equal parts of greens, carrots, spinach, broccoli, apples, brown rice, or cooked cornmeal.

Preparation: Rinse the vegetable ingredients and the chicken eggs or shrimp well under running water. Puree these ingredients, adding a little water, to form a thin mash with the consistency of honey. Do the same with the meat ingredients, then mix everything well. Heat the mash to 175°F (80°C) (check the temperature with a food thermometer). For each generous quart (one liter) of mash, add one level teaspoon of vitamin/mineral supplement (see page 39).

Stir the mash constantly while it cools to 140°F (60°C). Now add a high-quality gelatin powder, following package directions for aspic. (Inferior aspic powder will not set the food properly.) Pour into a shallow pan or dish. After it sets, cut the aspic into daily portions, place in plastic bags, and freeze.

Water

It is important that clean water is available at all times for captive turtles. The water dish must be easy to drink from and shallow enough so that the turtle won't drown if it happens to fall in and overturn.

Checklist
Feeding Guidelines

1 Always feed semiaquatic and aquatic turtles in the water.

2 To determine the right amount: Let a young turtle (up to one year old) go without food for a day; an adult, for two days. Then weigh or measure a good amount of its favorite food. Feed the turtle until its first eagerness subsides, and it starts to eat more slowly or selectively. Stop feeding; calculate how much it ate. In future, feed only half this amount.

3 If food is frozen, thaw and bring to water temperature before feeding.

4 Weigh the turtle at regular intervals to monitor food intake. If the folds of the skin bulge out of its shell when it draws in its legs, it is too fat. Reduce the amount of food by about 30–40 percent, until the fat deposits under its skin are no longer evident.

5 Make changes gradually. To introduce a new healthy main food, mix a little in with the preferred food, then gradually increase the proportion.

Breeding Turtles

If given care appropriate to the species, most turtles will reproduce in captivity. You must remember not only to provide the female with vitamin and mineral supplements to permit her to form strong eggs, but also to have an area and enough food for the young when they hatch. Once the young begin feeding, you can find new homes for the ones you do not wish to keep.

Sexual Maturity

The ability to reproduce depends not only on the turtle's age, but also on favorable living conditions, which promote rapid growth and earlier sexual maturity.

Australian snake-necked turtles mate only underwater.

Many North American turtles breed when five years old.

European pond and river turtles are not sexually mature until they are 10–12 years old.

Many species reach reproductive age between these two extremes.

The mating season for tropical and subtropical turtles (subtropical = European and North American) is generally between the end of April and the end of May. The mating instinct is triggered in springtime by increasing day length.

Mating Behavior

Many of the semiaquatic turtles that spend most of their time on land begin their courtship there, in much the same way as land turtles, but prefer to perform the actual mating in the water. An example is the wood turtle (see page 10).

Aquatic turtles use the entire swimming area for their mating rituals. In many species of slider and painted turtles, a male with the urge to mate will approach the female with the forelegs extended, vibrating them about her face and neck and stroking her with his greatly lengthened foreclaws. Connected with this is a thorough preliminary investigation of the turtle's scent, which can be conducted even under water. Each species has a distinctive odor and courtship behavior; this almost completely rules out unsuitable pairings—that is, interspecies breeding—at least in the wild.

In other species, after the sniffing ritual, the male vigorously nods his head up and down. He bites at the female, which hides her head in her shell. Finally, the male grasps the edges of the female's shell with his claws as they copulate. By contrast, soft-shelled turtles engage in only mild foreplay.

Note: If the female remains unreceptive or the male's sexual drive is excessive, he may become so insistent that she can no longer eat or is injured by his biting. In that case, the male should be separated from the female for a few weeks.

The baby snake-necked turtle hatches after three months.

Fertilizing the Eggs

The male has already formed his sperm during the previous summer and stored them during hibernation.

The female establishes her eggs in summer and completes their development in springtime, after the winter rest. Before the shell is formed, the eggs are fertilized. This does not require mating each time; many females can store sperm for up to four years. Thus, it could happen that a turtle you acquire already grown, and keep by itself, would lay fertilized eggs after one to three years.

Breeding Tips

To breed turtles successfully, you must observe certain essentials:

✔ Offer hibernation on an individual basis, for turtles that belong to a hibernating species (see pages 10–17).

✔ If possible, keep a breeding pair in an outdoor enclosure during the summer months; successful breeding is almost guaranteed.

If you can't keep your turtles outdoors (either in the yard or on the balcony), you must make certain specific adjustments in the terrarium.

1. Separate the turtles for one to two months before you plan to breed them (keep them where they cannot see, hear, or smell each other), then reunite them. This is especially helpful for species that do not hibernate. This separation occurs naturally in hibernating species.

2. Three months before you want them to mate, decrease the artificial daylight provided by the overhead spot lamp and other terrarium lighting to just six hours a day. After two months, increase the lighting gradually, over three to four weeks, to a maximum of 12 hours daily.

3. Do the same with the temperatures in the terrarium. Three months in advance, at the same time as you reduce the lighting, lower the air and water temperatures by about 8–10°F (4–5°C) below the recommended upper limit. For example, if the recommended range is 75–79°F (24–26°C), reduce the temperatures to about 72°F (22°C). Turn off additional heat sources, such as spot lamps and underground heating mats.

4. As you extend the hours of daylight, gradually increase the temperature over three to four weeks. In the final week, turn on the overhead spot lamp as well, adding an hour a day.

5. If your turtles spend most of their time on land, in the final week give them a spring rain. Twice a day, spray the terrarium and the turtles with a plant mister. This increases the humidity. Higher humidity, along with the rising temperature, helps trigger the mating urge.

Note: It's best to use rainwater or softened water for misting. Otherwise, mineral deposits will form on the terrarium glass.

6. When you give your turtles fresh, tender food while increasing the temperature, they will surely know that spring has come; their courtship rituals will commence, and mating will soon follow.

Depositing the Eggs

All turtles lay their eggs on land. Therefore, you must make provisions for aquatic turtles to leave the water to deposit their eggs. Semiaquatic turtles will bury their eggs in an area of the terrarium with warm, slightly moist sand, if the sand is at least as deep as their shell length. Regardless of whether the species is aquatic, semiaquatic, or terrestrial, you must provide a suitable earthen nesting area.

Note: You will find instructions for preparing an egg-laying area for semiaquatic and aquatic turtles and using an artificial incubator in the "HOW-TO" section on pages 46–47.

Removing the Eggs

Carefully dig up the eggs and place them in small plastic containers half-filled with dampened vermiculite. Place the containers in an incubator.

Keeping turtles outdoors in warm weather makes it easier to breed them successfully.

Caring for Baby Turtles

It can take turtles one to three days to emerge from the egg. During this time, the eggs must not be disturbed.

Leave the hatchlings in the incubator for a few days, until the yolk sac on the navel has shriveled and fallen off. Of course, this requires an incubator of adequate size (see HOW-TO, page 46).

The hatchlings are raised separately from their parents. They need the same living conditions—light, temperature, and food—as the adult turtles. Baby turtles, however, do not eat immediately on hatching. It takes about a week for their metabolisms to adjust from digesting the yolk to digesting solid food. Mince their food somewhat smaller, so that the young turtles can grasp it easily. Provide the necessary calcium and vitamins (see page 39). Use caution in giving vitamins—too much is as harmful as too little, and your baby turtles might get sick (see page 51).

Note: In summer, you can feed young semiaquatic turtles live water-fleas, earth-worms, and tubifex worms (available at pet shops).

TIP

Are the Eggs Fertilized or Unfertilized?

To tell whether a turtle egg is fertilized, hold it upright (see page 46) between your thumb and forefinger in front of a bright light, such as a desk lamp. If the egg is fertilized, you will be able to detect blood vessels inside at an early stage, and later a darker area that grows as the turtle develops. Unfertilized eggs show two distinct areas; the very light area is the air pocket, and the somewhat darker region is the drying yolk. Also, fertilized eggs gain weight over time, whereas unfertilized eggs slowly lose weight as they dry up.

If a turtle embryo dies in the egg, don't assume that it's because of a mistake you've made during artificial incubation. A more likely cause is poor parental nutrition. If the parents receive an inadequate supply of vitamins or other essential nutrients, the embryo will be undernourished as well. A weak embryo may die in the egg even just before it was due to hatch. If this happens to eggs in your care, review your turtles' nutritional needs; in particular, be sure the female gets enough vitamins, trace elements, and natural sunlight.

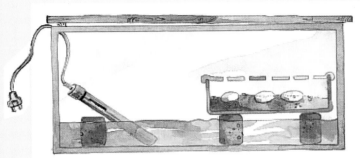

This setup offers ideal temperatures for incubating turtle eggs.

A Safe Incubation Chamber

In a plastic terrarium, place two bricks on their side. Add water to just below the top of the bricks. On the bricks, set the smaller plastic container of eggs (see above). Heat the water to 82°F (28°C) with an aquarium heater. Cover the aquarium with a pane of glass. A small wedge made of wood will allow the condensation to run off.

A *temporary incubation chamber* can be fashioned from a clay flowerpot filled with sand. Nest the eggs in the sand as described on page 47 and cover the flowerpot with a pane of glass. A wooden match inserted between the glass and the edge of the flowerpot provides ventilation. Keep the sand

For a temporary incubation chamber, fill a flowerpot with sand and cover it with a pane of glass.

slightly moist by setting the pot on a saucer containing a little water. Put the flowerpot in a warm room [80°F (27°C)]. This arrangement will keep the eggs from drying out until you can provide a safe incubation chamber.

Provide an Egg-laying Area

Semiaquatic turtles: For an improvised egg-laying area, use a plastic mortar pan (see drawing, page 36) half-filled with sand. Place it in a warm room in a spot that gets some sunlight, and let the turtle dig a hole for her eggs. A board covering half the pan creates a cave effect that gives the mother turtle a sense of security as she deposits the eggs. If conditions are right, semiaquatic turtles also will bury their eggs in the terrarium.

Aquatic turtles: Fill a box with sand and place it next to the aquarium in such a way that the turtle can leave the water and crawl up a ramp into the box. The sand should be at least as deep as the turtle's shell is long. Provide barricades (for example, of plexiglass), to ensure that the mother turtle won't fall out (see drawing on next page).

After the eggs are laid, you should remove them. Mark the top of each egg (there may be as many as six or more) with a soft lead pencil. They must not be turned for the rest of the incubation period; otherwise, the yolk will crush the embryo, and it will die.

run off the lid at an angle. Once you place this container in the aquarium described on page 46, monitor the humidity in the aquarium with a hygrometer hung by a wire on the aquarium wall. If the hygrometer shows a humidity of 95–100%, you may dispense with the lid on the inner incubation box.

Aquarium for water turtles, with egg-laying box. The turtle can climb up a ramp into the box. The plexiglass barricade keeps her from falling out.

It is also helpful to number the eggs, if they are laid at relatively long intervals. This will allow you to calculate when you can expect the hatchlings to emerge.

The incubation box starts with a clear plastic container. Cover the bottom with water 1/5 inch (5 mm) deep and fill the container halfway with vermiculite (from the hardware store). Bury the eggs halfway in the vermiculite, and cover the container with a lid that fits. The humidity inside will rise to the 100-percent level that is needed.

Lift the lid once a day, and fan a little fresh air into the container. To keep condensation on the underside of the lid from dripping onto the eggs (which can kill the embryos), tilt the container, setting one edge on a matchbox or similar object, so the condensation can

Note:

The baby turtles hatch after 30 days (for soft-shelled turtles) or as long as 90 days (for painted turtles) or even 150 days (for snake-necked turtles).

Many species deposit all the eggs at once, others at intervals of 5 to 14 days.

Preventive Care and Health Problems

Most health problems that turtles develop in captivity arise from improper care. The three main causes of illnesses are drafts (see page 35), inadequate heat sources (see pages 21–25), and an incorrect diet, with calcium and vitamin deficiencies or overdosage (see pages 38–41). Poor hygiene can also cause severe illnesses.

Important Hygiene Measures

Semiaquatic turtles: Water basins and the damp sand around them are perfect refuges for parasites, their eggs and larvae, and bacteria such as salmonella. For this reason, it is essential to scrub the water basin, and change the water every day. Keep the soil around it dry. The best way to do this is to cover it with flat stones, which are warmed by the terrarium's heating system (see pages 21–25).
Change the sand around the bathing pool often (every four to eight weeks, as needed).

Aquatic turtles: In an aquarium, clean water is the most important requirement; feces and food remnants can drastically reduce the water quality and make the turtle sick. Keep a small number of turtles in as much water as possible. Thoroughly remove all food scraps and feces. Install a filter with good filtering capacity and keep it clean (see page 25).

Turtles and Your Health

Amoebas and many other parasites live in the bodies of turtles and other coldblooded animals. However, these parasites are unable to survive in the human body, which maintains a constant internal temperature of about 98.6°F (37°C). For this reason, the risk of transferring disease is very slight. If you keep your turtle free of worms, have its stool samples tested for parasites twice a year, keep its living quarters properly clean, and wash your hands after handling your turtle or the terrarium, there is no risk to your health.

Common Health Problems

Your turtle can't use its voice to let you know if it is sick or in pain. It's up to you to watch your pet carefully. Changes in behavior, such as apathy or loss of appetite, or external symptoms, such as swollen eyelids, indicate that your turtle may be sick. You should take it to the veterinarian at once.

A healthy turtle that has flipped onto its back can right itself without your help.

A baby big-headed turtle—a rare sight.

Diarrhea

Symptoms: Loose, slimy stools. Blood in the feces is cause for alarm.

Possible causes: Improper diet, protozoal or fungal infection, worms.

Treatment: Take the turtle to the veterinarian at once, with fresh stool samples (see page 31). Only a veterinarian can determine the cause of the problem.

Respiratory Distress

Symptoms: With extended neck and gaping mouth, the turtle makes cheeping, moaning, or snoring sounds; in between, it lowers its head in fatigue. Water turtles spend most of the time under the heat lamp, breathing with the mouth open.

Possible causes: Lung infection; constipation; difficulty laying eggs (see page 51); gas in the stomach or intestines; bladder stones or uric acid calculus, preventing evacuation of the anal bladder; edema caused by kidney or heart disease.

Treatment: Do not add additional warmth! This would raise the turtle's metabolism, which can be acutely life-threatening! You should take your turtle to the veterinarian at once. **Note:** Fungal, bacterial, or herpes infections can cause the mouth to be coated with substances that inhibit breathing. Herpes in turtles is usually fatal. Only immediate quarantine, sanitary measures, and disinfection can save the other turtles.

Open wide! The Mississippi map turtle reaches for a tempting morsel.

Swollen Eyes

Cause: Foreign bodies in the eye, injuries, drafts, vitamin A deficiency.

Vitamin A deficiency occurs almost only in aquatic turtles. It causes an increased exfoliation of cells of the harderian glands above the eyes. The eyelids become filled with an opaque white mass of conglutinated cells. The turtle cannot see, and it stops eating. Its eyelids bulge like a frog's, and it repeatedly rubs at its eyes with its front legs.

Treatment: Only by a veterinarian, who will rinse the turtle's eyes with a small syringe and possibly inject vitamin A. For prevention, be sure your turtle eats a varied diet (see pages 38–41).

Shell Injuries

Cause: Usually accidents.

Treatment: Superficial abrasions of the horny layer are harmless. However, if the wound is so deep that it reaches the bone, the turtle must be taken to the veterinarian, who will remove the infected tissue and treat the bone wound daily.

Mineral Deficiency

Symptom: The turtle eats sand or gravel in large quantities.

Possible cause: Mineral deficiency.

Treatment: Change the substrate to large, 1" pebbles or waterproof astroturf. Provide vitamins, calcium, and trace elements (see page 39). Eating sand and gravel can cause fatal obstructions.

Vitamin A Overdosage

Symptom: Shedding, until the skin is raw.

Treatment: Only by a veterinarian. The turtle must be kept very clean (risk of infection) and fed well. Screen to protect against flies in the terrarium or aquarium. Gently coat the wounds with healing ointment.

Avoid vitamin A preparations for several months.

Vitamin D₃ Overdosage

Symptoms: The turtle's shell becomes soft, with bleeding at the seams between scutes.

Treatment: Veterinary attention is needed. Handle the turtle very gently. Provide regular mineral supplements. Do not allow access to sand and gravel. Grind boiled eggshells and sprinkle them over the turtle's food. Use vitamin D₃ only in low doses and provide regular ultraviolet light (see pages 21–25).

Difficulty Laying Eggs

Symptoms: Unsuccessful digging and unproductive straining while laying eggs.

Possible causes: Mineral and hormone deficiencies can cause difficulty in laying eggs. Other possible causes include an egg that is too large, malformed eggs, a kinked or even twisted oviduct, obstruction by sand, injury to the cloaca, or a bladder stone.

Treatment: Only a veterinarian can treat this condition. Do not delay treatment.

Checklist
Caring for a Sick Turtle

1 Move a sick turtle to a quarantine terrarium/aquarium (see pages 30–31). Scrupulous cleanliness is essential.

2 Act immediately to correct any contributing factors such as drafts, cold, or improper diet.

3 If it is necessary to apply ointment, be sure the body part is clean and dry. Keep the turtle away from sand.

4 A sick or weak turtle may linger too long under the heat lamp or ultraviolet light, and this may lead to sunburn. If your pet is ill, limit basking to about five minutes a day.

5 Likewise, a turtle that spends too much time under an infrared light may become dehydrated. Ask the veterinarian how much infrared light is safe.

6 A disposable syringe (without a needle) is useful for administering liquid medications.

BEHAVIOR AND ACTIVITY

Turtles are usually silent, though you may hear hisses from a male during mating or noisy breathing from a turtle with a respiratory ailment. However, you can learn about their moods and feelings by watching what they do. To understand a turtle properly, it's essential to know about its natural behavior and activity.

Body Language

A turtle's body language can be very expressive. Turtles in captivity often exhibit the following behaviors:

Pacing or swimming back and forth: A turtle may cruise endlessly along the wall of its enclosure, or it may go to a corner and try to climb out over the edge. Similarly, an aquatic turtle may swim back and forth along the glass sides of the aquarium. This can be a clear signal that the turtle is not happy in its surroundings or that a female turtle needs an egg deposition site. Review the conditions your turtle needs (see Profiles, pages 10–17), and make any necessary adjustments. If a newly acquired turtle has just moved into its terrarium or aquarium, it may simply be curiously investigating its territory. After a day or two, however, the turtle should have calmed down.

Digging in the ground: If your female turtle keeps scraping at the ground with her hind legs and if her size is between half-grown and adult, she may be trying to lay eggs. This behavior can even be observed when there is no earth to dig in. For example, if you place the turtle on a smooth surface, she will still scrape and scratch. Immediately provide a suitable place for the turtle to deposit her eggs (see pages 46 and 47).

Stretching out flat on all fours: The turtle extends its extremities, including its head and tail, as far as it can out of its shell. The head usually rests flat on the ground, eyes closed. This behavior can be seen especially outdoors in the sunshine and under the overhead spot lamp in the terrarium or aquarium. Your turtle is sunbathing.

Caution: If your turtle spends all day in this position under the heat lamp or ultraviolet lamp, you should be concerned. Pick up the turtle to see if it actively assumes a defensive posture. If it does not, but instead seems to be listless, it is probably sick and must be taken to the veterinarian.

Basking in the garden pond, a painted turtle takes advantage of a sunny day.

Standing tall, legs extended, head held high: Your turtle is curious and is taking this posture to get a better look around. On land, this position also makes it easier to defecate.

Pulling in the head and legs: If the turtle suddenly pulls in its head and legs, it has been alarmed.

On land, a semiaquatic turtle rams another with its shell: The aggressor may approach diagonally from the front, perhaps nipping at the other turtle's legs or neck. A male turtle often does this as a prelude to mating. The male is signaling the female to hold still, lie down, and accept his advances. If the aggression leads to injuries, you should separate the turtles.

A land-dwelling semiaquatic turtle burrows into hiding in its terrarium: If it also stops eating, the turtle may be showing signs of preparing to hibernate. This happens in autumn, when the days are much shorter and the sun is low in the sky. At other times of year, however, such behavior may indicate that the turtle is ill. In that case, take the turtle to the veterinarian at once.

The Senses

The sense of smell is highly developed, leading a turtle unerringly to a suitable mate and to its feeding spot. The smell of a particular food is a critical factor in determining whether a turtle will like it. Aquatic turtles can smell just as well under water as on land, and they also use their sense of smell to navigate. By moving the floor of the mouth, they pump water through the nose into the mouth and let it flow out of the mouth.

Vision is very keen, enabling turtles to detect food and enemies from afar. For example, an eastern box turtle can spy a cricket or snail from a great distance. When nearby, however, it tends to rely more on its sense of smell. Many turtles can also recognize a familiar person from far away and will come closer.

Hearing is less acute. Turtles hear low-pitched sounds best. A turtle also senses vibrations (footsteps, falling rocks) in the ground; the vibrations are conducted through the legs and shell to the inner ear. Turtles do not have an external ear; the eardrum lies directly below the skin. For this reason, it is often difficult to identify the ear. The ear is located slightly behind the jaws and is often covered by leathery skin or by scales.

The Turtle's Shell

A turtle's most striking feature is its shell. For the most part, the shell consists of living material that can be injured.

An older musk turtle can be quite aggressive.

Bony plates constitute the supporting structure of the shell, made up of areas of ossified skin, fused together with parts of the vertebrae, ribs, and shoulder girdle. The shell is thus an integral part of the turtle's skeleton. This vaulted bone structure is covered by a sensitive membrane of connective tissue, which is protected only by the horny shield plates. These horny plates, the *scutes*, are the only parts of the shell made of dead tissue, comparable to that of a human's fingernails. **Note:** The individual scutes are joined by growth areas, usually lighter in color. Here, the horny layer is much thinner and offers little protection. These regions are highly sensitive, and they should not be scratched, probed with a fingernail, or scrubbed with a brush. A turtle's shell may grow more bumpy with age, and the scutes may thicken. However, the scutes wear down uniformly as the turtle rubs against roots and stones in its wanderings or as it burrows into the ground.

Hinged joints are another distinctive feature of turtle shells, as seen in the box turtles (page 15). This modification carries the shell's protective function to amazing perfection. A more typical turtle—for example, the red-eared slider—pulls its head, arms, and legs into its shell, leaving the tough skin of its legs exposed. The box turtle, however, can raise the front and rear sections of its plastron like a drawbridge, closing the shell up tight and offering complete protection all around.

The soft-shelled turtles have a distinctively reduced shell. The flat, bony carapace is covered only by a tough, leathery skin, with no scutes. The plastron consists of somewhat broader bones in the region of the hip and shoulder girdles. Most of the underbelly is thus covered only by soft skin.

An amazing feature is that a soft-shelled

TIP

Shedding of Horny Layers

Turtles of many aquatic species (including *Chrysemys*, *Cuora*, and *Chelodina*) may shed the upper layer of scutes at regular intervals. This is not a symptom of disease. In other species, particularly the more land-dwelling turtles, such shedding is a sign that the turtle is ill; consult a veterinarian.

turtle, buried in sand, can breathe through its skin, taking in oxygen and releasing carbon dioxide into the water. As a result, soft-shells are also very sensitive to dirty water in the aquarium or to shell injuries, which can quickly become infected.

The color of the shell may vary, depending on a number of different factors. Turtles of many species change shell color as they get older; the bright, fresh markings fade, or the basic shell color becomes darker. Captive turtles are almost always more uniform in color than those of the same age in their native habitat. The more brilliant and intense coloration of turtles in the wild can be attributed to the influence of natural sunlight and a more varied diet.

In any case, there's no need to worry if your terrarium- or aquarium-dwelling turtle's shell changes color.

BODY LANGUAGE: A GUIDE

Understanding your pet turtle is easier if you can interpret its behavior correctly.

 This is what my turtle is doing.

 What does it mean?

 Here's what to do!

 Head and limbs drawn in.
 The turtle is alarmed.
 Best to leave it in peace until it's ready to face the world again.

 Yum! Swallowing an earthworm.
 Aquatic turtles mainly seek out and eat their food under water.
 To feed aquatic turtles, scatter the food on the surface of the water.

 Topsy-turvy turtle.
 The turtle flails its legs to turn itself right side up.
 You don't usually need to help.

Some species of aquatic turtles have a "hook" on the upperjaw. They use this in climbing.

The "hook" must never be trimmed.

🖼️ The spotted turtle creeps onto the shore.

❓ It needs to move freely between water and land.

❗ Be sure the shore is gently sloping.

The turtle 👉 paddles slowly through the water.

❓ Foraging for food is good exercise.

❗ Give your aquatic turtle plenty of room to swim.

👆 Warily, the turtle pokes its head above water.

❓ It needs to feel secure in its surroundings.

❗ Keep a good distance away, and move slowly.

All four legs extended. 🖼️

This turtle is sunbathing. ❓

Even in the terrarium or aquarium, ❗ provide good basking spots.

👆 Head and neck tucked sideways into the shell.

❓ Snake-necked turtles do this when they sense danger.

❗ Watch and wait; your pet will relax when it feels safe.

HOW-TO: TRAIN A TURTLE

A turtle can be highly entertaining—just give it the right challenges.

Take Advantage of Its Natural Tendencies

If you take the time to observe your turtle carefully and interact with it regularly, you'll be surprised at how much it can entertain you. Turtles learn quickly; the key is to take advantage of their natural curiosity and, especially, their appetite.

You must provide the right conditions to meet your turtle's basic needs. This includes offering plenty of diversity in its living quarters (see pages 21–29).

Responding to sounds: Remember that turtles don't have particularly acute hearing; they are best able to hear low tones. You might be able to teach your turtle to respond when you ring a bell, for example, or play deep notes on a musical instrument. Always accompany the sound with a tasty treat, so that your turtle learns to associate the two. Use patience—but don't be disappointed if your turtle doesn't master this particular trick. Each turtle has its own personality, and many simply won't respond to bribery.

Hide and seek: In the wild, a turtle spends all day foraging for food. You can keep your pet turtle active by feeding it often—though you must be careful not to overfeed it (see page 41). Challenge your turtle's hunting instincts by offering live food (for young turtles, daphnia and mosquito larvae). Some live turtle food, such as tubifex worms, will even seek out hiding places under water. If you're tempted to feed your turtle live fish, consider that while this is natural for the turtle, some people may find it cruel.

Taming a Turtle to Your Touch

Observe your pet to see what foods it likes best.

Diving into the water is twice as much fun in pursuit of a tasty treat.

Take the treat between your thumb and forefinger and hold it out to your turtle; for aquatic turtles, hold it at the surface of the water. The turtle will first sniff cautiously at the food, which also smells a little like your hand. Then it will take a few tentative nibbles. Try not to make any sudden movements now, or you will startle your pet and make it wary of you.

Usually, however, most turtles soon become

Varied underwater terrain keeps a turtle active and fit.

accustomed to your hand and your person. In the future, your turtle will associate your arrival with something good to eat.

Note: It's hard to say how long it will take before a turtle is tame to your touch. Many turtles never lose their natural wariness.

Lying in wait. When will the next juicy mealworm drop?

A Mealworm Machine

This simple device will entertain your pet turtle and give it exercise as well. Take a plexiglass tube about 8 inches (20 cm) long, and drill a row of holes 5/64 inch (2 mm) in diameter along it. Hang the tube above the water with wires, holes down. Put several mealworms in the container, and plug each end with a cork. The mealworms will crawl along the tube until they discover the holes.

Then they will work their way out, falling into the water at irregular intervals. The turtle below will pounce on this unexpected snack. Because it doesn't know just when the next yummy tidbit will appear, it will hover watchfully nearby, then nimbly go after the mealworm when it drops.

Note: Mealworms are easy to raise at home, but you can also buy them at a pet store. Remember that these are treats, not the turtle's main food.

You can feed your turtle with tweezers, but this won't tame it to your touch.

Page numbers in bold print refer to color photos and illustrations.

The Reeves' turtle
originates in Asia and
does not hibernate.

Useful Addresses

California Turtle and Tortoise Club
P.O. Box 7300
Van Nuys, CA 91409

Desert Turtle Preserve Committee
P.O. Box 463
Ridgecrest, CA 93555

National Turtle and Tortoise Society
P.O. Box 66935
Phoenix, AZ 85082

The New York Turtle and Tortoise Society
163 Amsterdam Ave., Suite 465
New York, NY 10023

Other Resources

Talk to your pet store owner, staff at nature centers, and the faculty of any local university that offers herpetology courses.

Literature

USEFUL BOOKS

Conant, Roger and Joseph T. Collins. *Reptiles and Amphibians*, Eastern/Central North America. Boston: Houghton Mifflin, 1991.

Ernst, Carl H., et al. *Turtles of the United States and Canada*. Washington, DC: Smithsonian Institution Press, 1994.

Ernst, Carl H. and R. W. Barbour. *Turtles of the World*. Washington, DC: Smithsonian Institution Press, 1989.

USEFUL MAGAZINES

Reptile Hobbyist
One TFH Plaza
Neptune City, NJ 07753

Reptiles
P.O. Box 6050
Mission Viejo, CA 92690

Reptiles and Amphibian Hobbyist
RD3, Box 3709-A
Pottsville, PA 17901

About the Author

Dr. Hartmut Wilke studied marine biology and fisheries science at the Universities of Mainz and Hamburg, Germany. He did his doctoral research on diseases in fish. From 1973 to 1983, he was the director of the Exotarium at the Zoological Garden in Frankfurt am Main, Germany. Since 1983, he has been the director of the Vivarium Zoological Garden in Darmstadt, Germany. One of his areas of specialization is reptile breeding. He has more than 20 years of experience in the care of turtles and tortoises.

Acknowledgments

The author and the publisher wish to thank Mr. Rolf Warnecke for sharing his practical experiences from many years of turtle care, and Dr. Gisela Keil for contributing the chapter on "Preventive Care and Health Problems."

About the Photographer

The photographs in this book were taken by Uwe Anders, except for those taken by Kahl (page 17, top left); by Reinhard (page 10, bottom, and page 50); and by Silvestris (page 13, bottom).
Uwe Anders has a degree in biology and has been active for many years as a freelance nature photographer and a cameraman for nature film productions. He writes articles on nature, and he lectures at various institutions about nature photography and travel photography. His photographs appear in several pet owner's guides published by Barron's Educational Series.

About the Artist

Robert Fischer has a degree in graphic design; he lives and works in Munich, Germany. His portfolio includes such diverse works as detailed nature studies, illustrations of fairy tales, and computer collages.

Photos on Book Cover, Title Page, Chapter Title Pages:

Front cover: Red-eared slider (large photo); wood turtle (small photo).
Back cover: Yellow-bellied slider.
Page 1: Painted turtle.
Pages 2–3: American redbelly turtle (Pseudemys rubiventris), photographed in the wild in Florida.
Pages 4–5: Common musk turtle, or stinkpot.
Pages 6–7: Red-eared slider.
Page 64: wood turtle.

Important Note

Caution should be exercised before using any of the electrical equipment described in this book.

While handling turtles you may occasionally receive bites or scratches. If your skin is broken, see your physician immediately.

Some terrarium plants may be harmful to the skin or mucous membranes of humans. If you notice any signs of irritation, wash the area thoroughly. Turtles may transmit certain infections to humans. Always wash your hands thoroughly after handling.

Publication Data:

English translation
© Copyright 2000 by Barron's Educational Series, Inc.
Original title of the book in German is *Wasser Schildkröten*
© Copyright 1998 by Grafe and Unzer, Verlag GmbH, Munich

All inquiries should be addressed to:
Barron's Educational Series, Inc.
250 Wireless Boulevard
Hauppauge, New York 11788
http://www.barronseduc.com

ISBN-13: 978-0-7641-1183-9
ISBN-10: 0-7641-1183-3

Library of Congress Catalog Card No. 99-38994

Library of Congress Cataloging–in–Publication Data
Wilke, Hartmut, 1943–
[Wasser Schildkröten. English]
    Turtles: a complete pet owner's manual: everything about purchase, care, nutrition, behavior, and breeding/Harmut Wilke;
illustrations by Robert Fischer.
        p.   cm.
    Includes bibliographical references (p.   )
    ISBN 0-7641-1183-3 (alk. paper)
    1. Turtles as pets. I. Title.
SF459.T8W5613   2000
639.3'92—dc21   99-38994
                                                          CIP

Printed in China
19 18 17 16 15 14

1 Should a turtle be allowed to hibernate in a garden pond?

Not in latitudes where the autumn and winter are long and cold. The risk of harming the turtle's health is too great.

2 Sometimes my turtle extends all its legs. What is it doing?

It may be sunbathing. This position also makes it easier to defecate.

3 My turtle has begun swimming constantly back and forth along the aquarium wall. What does this mean?

If your pet is a half-grown or adult female, she may be seeking a place to lay eggs. Turtles also respond in this way if their living conditions have deteriorated.

4 My turtle is less than one year old. Will it still survive the hibernation period?

It may not. As long as your turtle is healthy and active, it may not need to hibernate.

5 One of my two turtles keeps hovering with its front legs extended and quivering in a very odd way.

This is courtship behavior. A male turtle will even approach another male in this way, in the absence of a suitable female.